THE
POCKET

Billie
Eilish

Published in 2024
by Gemini Adult Books Ltd
Part of Gemini Books Group

Based in Woodbridge and London

Marine House, Tide Mill Way,
Woodbridge Suffolk, IP12 1AP
United Kingdom
www.geminibooks.com

Text and Design © 2024 Gemini Adult Books Ltd
Part of the Gemini Pockets series

ISBN 978 1 80247 265 3

A CIP catalogue record for this book is available from the British Library.

Disclaimer: The book is a guidebook purely for information and
entertainment purposes only. All trademarks, individual and company
names, brand names, registered names, quotations, celebrity names,
logos, dialogues and catchphrases used or cited in this book are the
property of their respective owners. The publisher does not assume
and hereby disclaims any liability to any party for any loss, damage
or disruption caused by errors or omissions, whether such errors or
omissions result from negligence, accident or any other cause. This
book is an unofficial and unauthorized publication by Gemini Adult
Books Ltd and has not been licensed, approved, sponsored or endorsed
by Billie Eilish or any other person or entity.

Printed in China

Cover illustration by Natalie Floss

10 9 8 7 6 5 4 3 2 1

Images: © Alamy: 7 /Jeffrey Mayer;. 40 /Doug Peters; 104 /Jason
Richardson. © Getty Images:.8 /Steve Granitz; 76 /Michael Hickey. ©
Shutterstock: 4 /Lanang Banget.

THE
POCKET

Billie
Eilish

G:

CONTENTS

Introduction

Billie Eilish is unlike any other artist on the modern pop landscape. A genre-less, paradigm-splitting shape-shifter whose music is as sinister as it is subversive, as happy as it is hilarious. Billie's a disrupter, a game-changer, a content creator who has captured that creeping feeling we all sense about the world today and distilled it into a stunning run of mind-altering meta-music, the skill of which should be beyond her years, but magically isn't. In short: Billie is the brain-tingling sound of now.

Welcome to the pocket-sized pick-me-up of the biggest pop star on the planet – Billie Eilish.

Chapter One
New Wave

Billie Eilish

Happy Birthday Billie (& Brad!)

On 18 December 2001, just three months after
the shocking and tragic events of 9/11 in New
York, Billie was born in a hospital local to her
family home in Highland Park, California. Billie's
parents, Maggie Baird and Patrick O'Connell,
were overjoyed to have a daughter, though they
consider themselves to be "late parents" as
they didn't have Billie until their mid-forties,
four years after their first-born, Finneas.

Billie shares her birth date with several famous
music artists and Hollywood players, such as
Christina Aguilera, Katie Holmes, Ray Liotta,
DMX, Betty Grable, Keith Richards, Steven
Spielberg, Sia and, perhaps most famously,
Mr Brad Pitt.

No Way!

On the day Billie was born, the No.1 song in the US was the popular but often ridiculed 'How You Remind Me' by Nickelback. (We could argue Billie was born to save the world from bands like Nickelback!)

"The One with the Mother on *Friends*"

Billie's mother, Maggie, an actress and screenwriter, made an appearance in the hit TV show *Friends* two years before she gave birth to Billie. In the 1999 episode "The One Where Joey Loses His Insurance", Maggie played "casting director number two" and asked Joey (Matt LeBlanc) to pick up a bag of pet food while auditioning for an advert.

" I was 13 when this started, so I didn't know anything. I'd go into meetings and they'd say, 'So Billie, what do you think?' and I'd just be like, 'Am I supposed to know? Because I don't.' But eventually I got the hang of it. And now in the meetings I have I explain every single detail of every single thing that I'm thinking; and people do it! "

Billie, interview with Mark Savage,
BBC, 15 July 2017

18 November 2015

The day Billie and Finneas's lives changed forever was the day Billie uploaded 'Ocean Eyes' to Soundcloud late on a Wednesday evening. "Screw it. Let's just put it out now," Billie told Finneas. It was Finneas who wrote the song originally for his rock-pop band The Slightlys, but with them it never sounded how Finneas heard in his head. "I'm failing the song," he told the *Rolling Stone Music Now* podcast in December 2021. So, in October 2015, Finneas walked into Billie's bedroom and asked her to sing it.

"I'd heard it because I was right next door," Billie told *Vogue* in 2017. "I sang it, and we both loved it. I couldn't get it out of my head for weeks. It's just a beautiful song. Finneas is an amazing writer."

*

'Ocean Eyes' was released precisely one year later – on 18 November 2016 – through her record label, Darkroom/ Interscope Records.

Light in the Dark

In August 2016, the first big domino in Billie's quest for world domination toppled, starting a chain reaction that we all enjoy today. Billie signed her dream-come-true record deal with Darkroom/Interscope Records, one of the US's most respected labels and home to many of the world's greatest musical artists, including Olivia Rodrigo.

It was Justin Lubliner, a 24-year-old executive at Interscope that first saw Billie's prolific potential. As Billie told *Billboard's* Lyndsey Heavens, on 5 November 2020:

"Justin was the only record label person out of everyone I met that year – and I met with a lot of people – that really saw something and believed it ...
He didn't have some plan to turn me into something different. He really just saw me for exactly who I was and wanted to support that. I think that's rare."

The Pirate

Billie's surname, Eilish, is actually her middle name. Before she was born, her parents named her Eilish after watching a documentary about conjoined Irish twins, Katie and Eilish Holton. They loved the name – Eilish is Gaelic for Elizabeth – and both Maggie and Patrick are from Irish and Scottish descent. However, Billie's grandfather, Bill, passed away just before Billie was born so she was named after him first: Billie Eilish Pirate Baird O'Connell.

Finneas, who was 4 when Billie was born, called his sister "Pirate" during Maggie's pregnancy, because he loved pirates. The name stuck enough to become part of Billie's legal birth name. While a fan of her pirate side, Billie has always seriously disliked her legal last name – O' Connell, from her father's side. "It sounds like if a goat was a person – Billie Goat O'Connell!" she told Josh Eells in a 2019 interview with *Rolling Stone*.

A Home Full of Music

Billie's family home in Highland Park, California, was always filled with the sound of music and songs being written. "I feel like I always wanted to write songs just because my brother did, and also my mom did," Billie told *Harper's Bazaar* in October 2017. "She taught both of us how to write and so I always have high standards for writing. If I didn't, I'd have 2,000 songs!"

Surrounded by instruments in such a tiny space – there were three pianos, including a grand that Billie's father picked up for free off the Internet, Maggie's guitar and a ukulele – it was no surprise when Billie began writing songs in her tweens. Famously, the O'Connell household had one night-time rule: no one would ever force you to go to sleep if you were playing music. As Billie was afraid of the dark, and her own dreams, she would stay up late practising her songwriting and video editing in her bedroom, skills she has now mastered.

Billie's favourite band of all time is The Beatles. When Billie headlined Glastonbury in 2022, so too did Beatle Paul McCartney, the night after. "I'm headlining the same festival as Paul McCartney... are you kidding me? The Beatles raised me. I owe 95 per cent of my love of music to the Beatles and Paul. It's insane to think about," she told the *NME* in June 2022.

Throughout her singing career, Billie has sung many Beatles songs, each time putting her own Billie-spin on them. At her first live performance at age 7, she sang 'Happiness Is a Warm Gun'. In 2019 on "Carpool Karaoke", she sang 'I Will' on the ukulele, and at the Academy Awards 2020, she sang a stunning version of 'Yesterday' during a very poignant In Memoriam section.

"I always say it was actually The Beatles who taught them to write songs."

Maggie Baird, about her children,
Far Out, February 2022

"There are still people who are afraid of successful women, and that's so lame. What's the point of pleasing other people? You've got to get out and change the world, and we're the generation that's going to step into that."

Billie Eilish, *Los Angeles Times*, 2018

Generation Z

Billie belongs to Gen Z, currently the largest generation in the history of the world, with more than 20 per cent of the US born between 1997 and 2012. Other extraordinary Gen Z-ers are Zendaya, Greta Thunberg and Olivia Rodrigo, to name just a few.

Maggie & Patrick

"No disrespect, but they weren't famous actor celebrities. They were working actors."

Billie, on her parents, soapcentral.com, November 2019

In the 1990s, Billie's mother, Maggie, was a member of the highly influential and inspirational Los Angeles improv and sketch comedy group, The Groundlings. While there, Maggie performed with actors who would later become world-famous, including Will Ferrell, Kristen Wiig and Melissa McCarthy. Billie's dad, Patrick, was an actor who had small roles in *The West Wing* and *Iron Man*.

" Billie and I often write lyrics and melody at the same time; sometimes we write lyrics before we write melody. But in this song's case, we wrote all of the melody before we wrote the lyrics, just because I had this feeling that the lyrics could be perfect, but if the melody isn't also perfect, then it's not going to land. "

Finneas, on writing 'No Time to Die', interview with Chris Willman, *Variety*, 3 December 2021

On 11 April 2017, Billie finally kept her fans waiting no more and released her debut EP *Don't Smile at Me*. "My EP is called *Don't Smile at Me* for a lot of reasons, but one of them would be when someone tells you, 'Why aren't you smiling? It's so much more beautiful when you smile.' I'm not gonna look like anybody except what I am. I want to impress myself," she told *Ssense* in 2017. The EP sold more than 2.5 million copies globally and was re-released later in the year to include the final three tracks.

In early January 2019, *Don't Smile at Me* was the first EP to reach 1 billion streams on Spotify.

Don't Smile at Me

1. 'Copycat'
2. 'Idontwannabeyouanymore'
3. 'My Boy'
4. 'Watch'
5. 'Party Favor'
6. 'Bellyache'
7. 'Ocean Eyes'
8. 'Hostage'
9. '&Burn' (with Vince Staples)
10. 'Lovely' (with Khalid)
11. 'Bitches Broken Hearts'

Billie's First Big Gig

While The 1975 may hold a special place in Billie's heart for being not only one of her favourite-ever bands, but also her second-ever gig; the honour of Billie's first big arena gig goes to, of course... Justin Bieber!

The Boy Wonder performed at Los Angeles Staples Center on 25 June 2013 when Billie, a 12-year-old tween, was in attendance. (Bieber himself wasn't much older to be fair, perhaps only 19 years old.)

As it was Billie's first gig, she attended the show with her mother, Maggie. During the high-octane performance, part of his globe-trotting Believe Tour, Justin performed many of his biggest hits, including Billie's favourite song of his from her childhood, 'As Long as You Love Me'.

School's out Forever

The "most boring" subject Billie once hated being quizzed about by the media and her fans was her home-schooling. As a child, Billie's parents decided to teach both Billie and Finneas at home. Maggie, Billie's mother, had a technique called strewing, where she would lay certain items, or books, on the floor and whichever one Billie picked up is what they would study that day. The process gave Billie the freedom to pursue her own interests, such as video editing, dance choreography and learning instruments, including the ukulele and piano, as well as allowing her parents to spend more time with their children.

"I've never been to school.
I grew up home-schooled,
stayed home-schooled, never
was not home-schooled.
I still learned everything, you
know? But I learned it in life."

Billie, interview with *Pitchfork*, November 2020

The Zombie Apocalypse

Billie first started writing songs when she was just 11 years old, though she has spoken of writing songs as far as back as 4 years old. However, her first "real" attempt came together for a song called 'Fingers Crossed'.

The lyrical theme is a zombie apocalypse. Billie took the inspiration from watching episode four of season four of *The Walking Dead*, which along with *Psych* and *The Office* are her favourite TV shows. In that episode, the character Bob Stookey utters the famous line "Everybody makes it 'til they don't", which makes up the song's haunting and sinister chorus. "I literally just watched *The Walking Dead* and I took little lines from it," Billie told Erica Gonzalez in a *Harper's Bazaar* interview in October 2017.

Psychopathic Pop

Following 'Ocean Eyes' was no easy task. Thankfully, Billie and Finneas had 'Bellyache', the first proper single from the *Don't Smile at Me* EP, released on 24 February 2017. It remains the song that defines Billie: darkly comic, hugely melodic.

The song's genesis began when Billie was sitting in her garage at home rehearsing for a show with Finneas's friends. "Finneas started riffing on the guitar, and I sang the first line 'Sitting all alone, with a mouthful of gum in the driveway.' Then my brother sang, 'My friends aren't far, in the back of the car' and I was like 'Lay their bodies,' like I had killed them!" Billie told the BBC's Mark Savage in July 2017.

"A couple of days later Finneas wrote the chorus, and the last line was, 'And now I got a bellyache'. It's such a childish line. But it's about someone who knows they're a psychopath."

An Evening with Billie Eilish

Billie's first-ever proper gig was at the Hi Hat club in Highland Park, California, on 10 August 2017. Billed as "An Evening with Billie Eilish", Billie performed for 40 minutes, singing the majority of the tracks from her *Don't Smile at Me* EP. Fans, and friends, lined up around the block dressed in either red or yellow – the EP's primary colours – to attend the sold-out show.

Kevin Bronson, for BuzzBands.la, reviewed the gig under the heading, "Billie Eilish proves to be more than just kid stuff at the Hi Hat" with the quote, opposite.

❱❱ It was like a bunch of teenagers took over an adult's clubhouse and had a blast. Playing Thursday to a room populated by a lot of friends, she said all the right things and sang all the right ways. Inhabiting her songs, she comports herself far beyond her years, her voice ranging from airy and wafer-thin to rich and dusky, as the material dictates. Bantering with her contemporaries, she's one of them. She even proved poised, acknowledging some important adults in the room. ❱❱

Chapter Two
Like, for Real

The End of the Beginning

When Billie was 11 her dreams of becoming a professional and competitive dancer were put on ice when she suffered a terrible injury during a dance class. In July 2017, Billie told the BBC's Mark Savage: "It was really bad. My bone separated from my muscle in my hip. We were doing hip-hop and it just popped. I haven't really danced since, which has been horrible." The injury not only ended Billie's pro dance career, it also unfortunately kickstarted Billie's depression and a three-month phase of self-harming.

While mourning her future, Billie's other passion – music – thankfully provided her an outlet to pour her prolific artistic creativity and dance skills into, as seen in her music videos, most notably the 'Ocean Eyes' dance performance video and 'Lost Cause'.

Built in a Lab!

Billie was conceived after four attempts of In Vitro Fertilization (IVF) treatment. The first time she heard this fact was – unbelievably! – live on air on SiriusXM's *The Howard Stern Show* in September 2019. Stern couldn't believe his ears and declared, "You were built in a lab!" Billie was so shocked when her Dad joked he was "left alone in a dark room" to produce a "sample", Stern said: "Billie, you look like you're going to pass out."

"Fame is horrible.
It's worth it
because it lets
me play shows
and meet people,
but fame itself is
fuckin' dreadful."

Billie, interview with Cady Drell,
Marie Claire, 7 February 2019

The Mezzo-soprano

At age 8 Billie began singing in the Los
Angeles Children's Chorus. Billie's ability
to express herself through choral singing,
and training her mezzo-soprano voice in a
particular way, has helped her develop her
unique vocal technique and expose her to
different types of classical music. Choral
singing also taught Billie to protect her voice
and not "fuck it up by just screaming".

On the *Happier Than Ever* track 'Goldwing', Billie sings – in a capella! – one of her favourite classical chorale hymns, 'Hymn to the Dawn', composed by Gustav Holst, with words translated from ancient Sanskrit texts. Billie uses the hymn to begin the song before ending it abruptly and jumping into her customary eclectic dark-pop style. It's as inventive and as it is inspiring!

Hometown Glory

Over the last decade, Billie's childhood neighbourhood of Highland Park has been slowly gentrifying and becoming popular, allowing critics of Billie to incorrectly label her as "just another little rich girl from LA". But when Billie was a child growing up in the area, she remembers the terrifying sound of gunfire, sketchy locals and her parents frequently having no money to pay bills.

Located 8 miles (13 km) from Hollywood, Highland Park has been home to a surprisingly large number of influential and iconic musicians and creative artists, such as Beck, Jackson Browne, Zack de la Rocha, Diane Keaton, Marc Maron, Skrillex, Emily Wells, Alex Borstein, Billy Corgan, William Goldman, F. Gary Gray, Fred Savage, Harold Ramis, D.B. Weiss, Rachel Brosnahan and, perhaps most famously, Orson Welles, the acclaimed director of the movie consistently called the greatest ever made, *Citizen Kane*.

Tourette's Syndrome

Diagnosed when she was a child, Billie's Tourette's manifests itself through involuntary body movements known as tics, predominantly a slight bulging of her eyes and a twitching of her head. Certain events trigger her tics, such as math and stress. Billie's not the first famous neurodivergent person to experience Tourette's – Wolfgang Amadeus Mozart, Kurt Cobain, Lewis Capaldi, David Beckham and Seth Rogan all are known to have suffered versions of it. It's not all bad either, the condition comes with strong verbal skills, tenacity, creativity, empathy and hyper focus.

"A lot of my fans
have Tourette's, which made
me feel kind of more at home
with saying it, and also
I felt like there was a
connection there."

Billie, on *The Ellen DeGeneres Show*,
1 April 2019

Celebrity Crush

Over the course of her rise to fame, Billie has revealed many of her favourite childhood celebrity crushes, inspirations and icons. Perhaps the most significant revealed – so far! – was Billie's adolescent love for *Buffy the Vampire Slayer* actress, and icon of the 1990s, Sarah Michelle Gellar.

When Gellar heard the news of Billie's crush, she posted to Insta, "I'm dead. That's all. I'm not a child anymore, but I totally have a crush on @billieeilish OK." Seeing Gellar post in her Insta feed, Billie was quick to reply: "Um, oh my God."

❯❯ I didn't know I was coming out, but I kinda thought, wasn't it obvious? I didn't realize people didn't know. I've been doing this for a long time, and I just didn't talk about it. Whoops. I saw the article, and I was like, 'Oh, I guess I came out today!' It's exciting to me because I guess people didn't know, so it's cool that they know...
I am for the girls. ❯❯

Billie, *Vanity Fair*, 3 December 2023

On 29 March 2019, Billie released her debut album *When We All Fall Asleep, Where Do We Go?* It was the day that Billie, at age 17, became the first artist born after 2000 to have a No. 1 album around the world. It spent three weeks at No. 1 on the US Billboard chart and did not leave the Top 10 for the whole year! The album also went on to sell more than 7 million copies, and was crowned the biggest global album of the year. It was also streamed more than *6 billion times* on Spotify in its first 12 months alone.

When We All Fall Asleep, Where Do We Go?

1. '!!!!!!!'
2. 'Bad Guy'
3. 'Xanny'
4. 'You Should See Me in a Crown'
5. 'All the Good Girls Go to Hell'
6. 'Wish You Were Gay'
7. 'When the Party's Over'
8. '8'
9. 'My Strange Addiction'
10. 'Bury a Friend'
11. 'Ilomilo'
12. 'Listen Before I Go'
13. 'I Love You'
14. 'Goodbye'

Lucid Dreaming

The title of Billie's debut album was inspired by her ability to lucid dream, a phenomenon that allows people to realize they are dreaming and even take control of their dreams. Unfortunately, Billie also suffers from persistent and torturous night terrors, including visions of monsters under the bed, ensuring her nightmares are as real as her dreams. The title of the album comes from a lyric in 'Bury a Friend'.

\\ I immediately knew what the album was going to be about, what the visuals were going to be, and everything in terms of how I wanted it to be perceived... 'Bury a Friend' inspired what the album is about. \\

Billie, *Rolling Stone*, January 2019

The Killing of Oscar Grant

Every year on 18 October, Billie's now-iconic *Vanity Fair* interviews have asked her the same question: "What is your favourite movie?" Billie's answer has repeatedly been *Fruitvale Station*.

Like, for Real

Written and directed by *Black Panther*'s
Ryan Coogler and released in 2013, the
movie is about the final 24 hours of a
22-year-old African-American man called
Oscar Grant, portrayed by Michael B.
Jordan. Oscar Grant was killed on New
Year's Day 2009 by a Bay Area police
officer in Oakland, California, at Fruitvale
Station. The murder kickstarted the Black
Lives Matter movement that rippled
throughout the world when the police
officer was sentenced to time in prison for
involuntary manslaughter.

Songs in the Key of Billie

In December 2017, Billie treated her fans to the "Playlist of My Life" as part of one of the first cover interviews she did with *Teen Vogue*. If superfans want to know the songs that have soundtracked Billie's teenage life then there is no better place to start than right here...

Like, for Real

*   'The Motto' – Drake & Lil Wayne

*   'Off to the Races' – Lana Del Rey

*   'Na Na Na (Na Na Na Na Na)
    – My Chemical Romance

*   'Japanese Denim' – Daniel Caesar

*   'I'm a Fool to Want You'
    – Frank Sinatra

*   'Mr Brightside' – The Killers

*   'Garbage' – Tyler, The Creator

*   'As Crazy as It Is' – ZHU, A-Trak
    and Keznamdi

*   'Starring Role' – Marina

*   'Lovefool' – The Cardigans

*   'Waiting for the End' – Linkin Park

*   'Hold On' – SBTRKT (feat. Sampha)

Baggy Clothes

When Billie first appeared to the public in 2016 she deliberately dressed in clothes she described as "800 times bigger" than her. It was all part of her masterplan to avoid being sexualized by the media's male gaze. Her choice of clothing was always deemed controversial, a double standard in the music industry that she hopes to kill dead. As she told the *NME* in 2017, "If I was a guy and I was wearing these baggy clothes, nobody would bat an eye. There's people out there saying, 'Dress like a girl for once! Wear tight clothes, you'd be much prettier and your career would be so much better!' No it wouldn't. It literally would not."

"Sometimes I dress like a boy. Sometimes I dress like a swaggy girl. And sometimes I feel trapped by this persona."

Billie, interview with Jonathan Heaf,
GQ, 4 June 2020

"I just don't understand, why would you eat an animal if you could just eat some chips?"

Billie, Instagram, June 2019

Animal Love

An avid animal lover and vegan since she was 17, Billie is also the proud parent of two rescue pets: cat Misha and dog Pepper. (Pepper sadly passed away in 2023.) In 2020, Billie adopted a pit-bull, Shark, and a pet tarantula, who goes by the name Cools. Billie is an advocate for animal rights too. In 2019, she won a PETA Best Voice for Animals award for her online activism.

Billie's parents raised her vegetarian and she has remained so all of her life. Her old Instagram handle even used to be @wherearetheavocados. In a 2019 interview with *Rolling Stone*, Billie revealed that the one and only time she has eaten a living creature was when she swallowed an ant that had fallen into her glass of soy milk! That's nothing, of course, when you remember that time in the 'You Should See Me in a Crown' video when Billie let a real tarantula spider crawl out of her mouth. Thankfully, she didn't swallow it.

Billie Eilish

Bad Guy Does Good – Duh!

'Bad Guy' was biggest global single of the year in 2019, and Billie was the most successful artist. The song was streamed more than 2.8 billion times in 2019 – that's 8 million times a day! The song also sold 19.5 million copies, which equates to just than less half of all the 45 million singles copies Billie has sold to date.

The song was more than just a commercial smash hit; it also won tons of critical praise and awards, including Record of the Year and Song of the Year at the 62nd Grammy Awards in January 2020.

"'Bad Guy' is about people that are always lying about themselves," Billie revealed to *Heat* magazine in 2019. "I feel like pretty much all the rappers right now are lying, about how much money they have, and about their house and their clothes, etc. It's like, 'Shut up, you don't have this.' It's just annoying."

*

Did You Know?

'Bad Guy' is also responsible
for bringing back the slang term
"duh!" into popular usage. The
word first gained popularity in
1943 after it appeared in a
Merrie Melodies cartoon.

Scorpions in the Night

As a child Billie was incredibly anxious and suffered from crippling, life-changing separation anxiety. In interviews, the singer has described not being able to cope being away from her parents. Were they to leave for even a few minutes, Billie would descend down a rabbit hole of blind panic worrying about what would happen to them, as well as worry about what would happen to her and fear being forgotten.

A large part of Billie's anxiety during her pre-teen years stemmed from being afraid of the dark, believing monsters were under her bed, night terrors and sleep paralysis, conditions she told *OK!* magazine was "a serious form of torture" because "The whole night is terrifying and then I wake up." As a result Billie slept with her parents until she was 11. If she did sleep by herself and woke up, she would scream the house down, adamant that scorpions were crawling all over the floor. She later revealed that therapy helped her with the night terrors.

"I'm my own worst enemy. I'm the monster under the bed."

Billie, in an interview with Zane Lowe
for Apple Music, July 2023

Grammy Domination

One of the most memorable popular cultural milestones of the 21st century was when Billie dominated the 2020 Grammy Awards ceremony winning five out of the six awards she was nominated for, including the most coveted four awards of the night: Best New Artist, Record of the Year, Song of the Year and Album of the Year. The iconic photograph of her struggling to clutch all her awards unsurprisingly went viral itself. Billie's win also made her the first woman – and the youngest person ever – to win the four main Grammy categories, a feat that's going to be hard to beat by future artists.

" Blending in, I have never understood that at all. Why would you want to be in a room of people that look exactly like you? I don't know. What's the point of dressing like someone else? They're already dressing that way. Do your own stuff. I've always known what I want and who I wanted to be, what I wanted to wear and who I wanted to be seen as. "

Billie, interview with Rebecca Haithcoat, *Ssense*, 28 February 2018

Billie's Tour Rider

For Billie's six major tours she has politely asked that her official tour rider be stacked with several essential home comfort items that make her life on the road a little more bearable. After all, to date, Billie Eilish has performed more than 500 shows all around the world. On her first world When We All Fall Asleep tour, Billie had the following items present in her dressing room on the day of the show.

1. Schär (gluten-free brand from Germany) for peanut butter and jelly sandwiches
2. Crackers
3. Chips
4. Salsa and guacamole
5. Pineapple
6. Watermelon
7. Peanut-butter pretzels
8. Tajín (a spicy Mexican seasoning)
9. Lemonade
10. Chocolate milk
11. Poppi (a low-sugar probiotic sparkling soda)
12. Lots of ice
13. Lots of bottled water
14. Deodorant
15. Mouthwash
16. Hydrogen peroxide
17. Q-tips ("for them ears")
18. Earbuds
19. A speaker
20. Aquaphor face moisturizer

21. "All that, nothing else."

Billie's a Belieber

As we all know, Billie has been in love with Justin Bieber for most of her life. More than just a fan, Billie believed was genuinely in love with Bieber. So much so in fact that her parents considered taking Billie to therapy over how much pain she was in over her "Bieber-ness". "He was my first love and in my head he was in love with me," Billie revealed in a radio interview with KROQ. The pair have a lot in common: they were both discovered at 13 and both are multitalented musical prodigies.

Billie and Bieber met for the first time in April 2019 at Coachella festival, a dream Billie could not seem to believe had come true. After the meeting, Justin sent Billie a message. He wrote: "Your love for me touched my heart. You are so special, not for what you can do but for who you are – remember that. You are an idol to so many and I'm excited to watch you flourish. Embrace it all, Billie. You are great... but not greater than anyone."

Chapter Three
*Colour &
Shape*

Synaesthesia

On top of Billie's Tourette's, ADHD and night terrors, Billie (and Finneas) experience a neurological condition called synaesthesia, a rewiring of the brain that blends and heightens the senses when listening to music. It's an essential component to Billie's songwriting and her ability to visualize music in several shapes, smells and colours in her mind. For example, she has described visualizing Finneas as an orange triangle. And her song, 'Bad Guy', conjures up yellow, the number seven and "smells like cookies".

In the US, approximately one in 25,000 people are synesthetes like Finneas and Billie. Other famous artists, and inspirations of Billie, have it too, such as Pharrell Williams, Chris Martin, Mary J. Blige, Charli XCX, Beyoncé, Kanye West, Lorde, Olivia Rodrigo and Billie's idol, Marina Diamandis.

ASMR Icon

Billie's close-to-the-mic singing, with its layers and layers of otherworldly harmonies and tender, dream-like whispers, has become famous for triggering the neurological phenomena – and social media trend – known as ASMR, or Autonomous Sensory Meridian Response.

ASMR is triggered when aural sensations, such as Billie's voice – or the scraping of perfectly fried piece of chicken! – bring on a deeply relaxing feeling or "brain tingles", a pleasurable sensation on the scalp and down the back of the spine and neck.

In Billie's songs, and Finneas's deliberate ASMR-based production, Billie's softly sung, whisper-thin voice is the main instrument we hear, often ping-ponging in our headphones lulling us into a safe space. Billie's most popular ASMR song? It's got to be 'Everything I Wanted'.

One for the Dads

Billie's genre-less music not only defines Generation Z, it appeals to Generation X too. Billie has a plethora of famous rock star fans from Julia Roberts to Sarah Michelle Gellar. Even elder statesmen of rock 'n' roll adore her, including Radiohead's esteemed frontman, Thom Yorke. When he met Billie at Coachella in 2019, he told her, "You're the only one doing anything f*cking interesting nowadays." Afterwards, Finneas described the comment to Billie as "The coolest thing anyone's ever said to you."

Dave Grohl, legendary lead singer of the Foo Fighters and former drummer of Nirvana, is a huge fan too, as he posted to his Instagram on 14 February 2019.

"The connection Billie has with her audience is the same thing that was happening with Nirvana in 1991...

I went to go see Billy Eilish not too long ago. Oh my god man. Unbelievable. My daughters are obsessed with her. When I look at someone like her, I'm like rock 'n' roll is not even close to being dead."

The Book of Billie

On 11 May 2021, Billie released her first-ever book, *Billie Eilish*, a stunning visual narrative that features hundreds of never-before-seen childhood photographs from her family's photo albums, chosen by Billie herself. The images are accompanied by intimate memories of Billie's "real life" before she was famous, and proof that Billie's natural hair colour is blonde! Upon its publication, Billie called the book her most personal project to date.

"I'm the type of person if you tell me to stop doing something, I'm going to do the opposite."

Billie, interview with Thomas Smith, NME.com, 4 January 2019

Vanity Fair Q&A

On the same date every year – 18 October – since 2017, Billie has completed the same video interview with *Vanity Fair*, answering the same 10 questions. It has been a fascinating way to show how Billie has changed over the years... and how much she has stayed the same.

Colour & Shape

1. What advice would you give yourself a year from now?

2. What advice would you give yourself a year ago?

3. What's your favorite movie?

4. What's your favorite color right now?

5. What's your biggest regret?

6. What's the biggest thing you've learned?

7. What country would you love to visit?

8. How do you define your style in three words?

9. What's your philosophy?

10. What do you want to say to yourself in a year?

Her Strange Addiction

In an interview with Australian radio station Triple J, Billie revealed in detail her strange addiction – *The Office*! – and its lyrical inspiration for the song 'My Strange Addiction', which also samples the fan-favourite 'Threat Level Midnight' episode.

\\\ I've seen *The Office* 12 times now and counting. Every time I finish it, I start it immediately right after from the beginning again. I have episodes memorized, it's my therapy, my little escape. As stupid as that sounds, that show has gotten me through my whole life. It inspired the song 'My Strange Addiction', which is about having somebody be your addiction and feeling like you're suffocating because you want somebody so bad that it's like a sickness. And my strange addiction is *The Office*. \\\

"I wake up one day and decide to wear a tank top. Suddenly my boobs are trending on Twitter."

Billie, interview with Jonathan Heaf,
GQ, 4 June 2020

Billie Meets *The Simpsons*

In April 2022, Billie appeared in the iconic animated family sitcom, *The Simpsons*. In the short episode "When Billie Met Lisa", Billie discovers Lisa Simpson searching for a quiet place to practise her saxophone and invites her into her recording studio for a jam. Billie asks Lisa, "My parents really support me in my career. Is your dad supportive of you?" Lisa replies about her own dad, the beloved American icon Homer: "If you give him enough beer and a pair of earplugs, and then tell him that he can be in another room? No." Poor Homie!

Queen of Dragons

Billie's No. 1 passion may well be
music but her love of supercars comes
a close second. Her first-ever car was
a 2008 blue Mazda 5, an automobile
that represents rather brilliantly Billie's
humble origins. Of course, as Billie's
fame and fortune grew, so too did
Billie's fleet of cars.

Billie's most treasured possession is her black matte Dodge Challenger SRT Hellcat, nicknamed "Dragon". Billie's baby, Dragon has been on the artist's mind since she was a child and one of her first big purchases once she became famous. The car famously stars in the 'Everything I Wanted' video, directed by Billie. However, Dragon is just one of five luxury vehicles Billie takes great pride in showing off, including a Range Rover, a McLaren 600LT and a Koenigsegg Agera RS that Billie calls "The Queen".

Isn't She Lovely?

With more than 2 billion views on YouTube, Billie's biggest music video by far, and a fan favourite live, is the song 'Lovely'.

Released in collaboration with rapper Khalid on 19 April 2009, 'Lovely' is one of Billie's more upbeat songs – 114 beats per minute! – and received universal acclaim by critics and fans. Incredibly, the song's creation came about when Khalid went to Billie's house to simply hang out as friends, but ended up writing a hit song!

*

Billie revealed to Beats 1 DJ Zane
Lowe that she called the track
'Lovely' because it is a depressing
song that is about being happy
in being miserable. The video
features Billie and Khalid sealed
in a box, safe – but trapped –
from the outside world.

On 30 July 2021, Billie sent her second studio album *Happier Than Ever* out into the world. The date was significant as it is also Finneas's birthday. *Happier Than Ever* stayed on the US Billboard Hot 100 chart for 26 weeks and, to date, has sold more than 1 million copies. Critics praised the downtempo and thoughtful album for its lyrical maturity and themes of isolation, abuse and fame set against low-key but anthem-esque melodies.

Happier Than Ever

1. 'Getting Older'
2. 'I Didn't Change My Number'
3. 'Billie Bossa Nova'
4. 'My Future'
5. 'Oxytocin'
6. 'Goldwing'
7. 'Lost Cause'
8. 'Halley's Comet'
9. 'Not My Responsibility'
10. 'Overheated'
11. 'Everybody Dies'
12. 'Your Power'
13. 'NDA'
14. 'Therefore I Am'
15. 'Happier Than Ever'
16. 'Male Fantasy'

Under the Covers

"The first song I learned was a song by the Beatles which is called 'I Will'," Billie told James Cordon on an episode of his "Carpool Karaoke". Billie then performed the track on ukulele and it was magnificent. In other interviews Billie confessed that she has been singing and performing the song 'I Will' since she was just 6 years old.

Other cover songs that Billie used to perform include around her family home was 'Tomorrow' from the *Annie* musical, and, of course, 'Hotline Bling' (on ukulele!) by Drake. When Billie goes out on her world tours, she is armed with even more covers too, of which we think these are her very best. Check them out:

* 'Smells Like Teen Spirit' – Nirvana

* 'Fallin'' – Alicia Keys

* 'Can't Help Falling in Love' – Elvis

* 'Call Me Back' – The Strokes

* 'You Don't Get Me High Anymore'
  – Phantogram

* 'Bad' – Michael Jackson

* 'Something' – The Beatles

* 'Sunny' – Bobby Hebb

* 'Fever' – Little Willie John

* 'Telegraph Avenue' – Childish Gambino

* 'Body Count' – Jessie Reyez

* 'I'm in the Mood for Love' – Julie London

Fall Asleep with Billie

Somewhat ironically, considering
the fact that Billie has endured
years of sleep paralysis and
night terrors, sleep scientists at
Denmark's Aarhus University voted
Billie's soothing and soulful synthy
sounds as the best to fall asleep to
after analyzing more than 200,000
songs from 985 Spotify playlists.

\\ When I was writing 'What Was I Made For?' I wasn't thinking about myself, or my life. I was just inspired by the perspective of a character. It was only afterward that I had a realization: It actually was about me. A lot of the time it is a subconscious thing, writing about myself, but doing it in a way that feels safer. It's kind of trippy. I was thinking about a character, but it turns out I am the character. \\

Billie, *Vanity Fair*, 7 December 2023

Me & Dad Radio

In May 2020, Billie launched her Apple Music show, an intimate, home-brewed series entitled "Me & Dad Radio". With Billie and her dad Patrick as the hosts, the pair "blabbed" around the subject of music and what inspires them. Billie told Zane Lowe in an interview with Apple Music in February 2020:

"My dad and I have had this relationship over the years of sharing music with each other... My dad has shown me some of my favourite songs in the world and I've shown him songs that he loves and adores also."

Over the course of the six-episode series, Billie and Patrick invited Maggie and Finneas in for banter too. The whole family shared their love of music and loads of revelations and hilarious insights into Billie and Finneas's life-less-ordinary. It's a must-listen show for any Billie superfan.

Chapter Four

Dreams & Nightmares

Lights! Camera! Billie!

Billie is a creative genius capable of conjuring music, video and movement in her mind as clearly as her synaesthesia allows her to smell colours. Billie has always relished the opportunity to apply her artistry to all areas of her career, including directing many of her own music videos, a passion and skill she learnt and developed while being home-schooled. As of April 2024, Billie has directed 11 videos of her own songs.

1. 'What Was I Made For?' (2023)
2. 'Male Fantasy' (2021)
3. 'Happier Than Ever' (2021)
4. 'NDA' (2021)
5. 'Lost Cause' (2021)
6. 'Your Power' (2021)
7. 'Therefore I Am' (2020)
8. 'Everything I Wanted' (2020)
9. 'xanny' (2019)
10. 'Bored' (2017)
11. 'Six Feet Under' (2016)

"Any time I'm creating anything I'm thinking about the video, I'm thinking about the artwork and I'm thinking about the colors. Everything that I make, I'm already thinking of what color it is, what texture it is."

Billie, interview with Josh Eells,
Rolling Stone, 313 July 2019

On 8 April 2024, Billie broke the Internet again
by announcing her brand-new album, her third,
entitled *Hit Me Hard and Soft*. Billie's Insta post
barely contained her pride and excitement:

"So crazy to be writing this right now. I'm nervy & excited… Finneas and I truly could not be more proud of this album and we absolutely can't wait for you to hear it. Love you love you love you."

In other big news, Billie also announced the album
would not feature any promotional or lead singles,
the first time the singer has adopted the strategy.
"I wanna give it to you all at once," she posted.

Hit Me Hard & Soft

1. 'Skinny'
2. 'Lunch'
3. 'Chihiro'
4. 'Birds of a Feather'
5. 'Wildflower'
6. 'The Greatest'
7. 'L'Amour De Ma Vie'
8. 'The Diner'
9. 'Bittersuite'
10. 'Blue'

Your Power

The song that Billie considers the favourite, and perhaps most important, out of all her songs she's written so far is 'Your Power', the first single from her 2021 album *Happier Than Ever*.

The song is very close to Billie's heart, as it is about the abuse of power she has witnessed or experienced as a female not only in the music industry but the world at large. She has said that singing the song makes her "feel vulnerable". She hoped the single's release could help change the systems that allow abuse to happen. "I really feel such a strong need to protect young people and young girls," she has said.

"There's a verse in 'Your Power' that is about my experience and that's as specific as I'll get."

Billie, *The Sunday Times*, 18 June 2022

Turning Red

As her star was rising worldwide, another dream of Billie's came true. In 2021, she and Finneas were asked to write and perform three tracks for Disney/Pixar's 2022 animated film *Turning Red*.

"When we got approached about this project, we leapt at the opportunity," Finneas said in the 'Panda Power' YouTube featurette that promoted the movie. The plot of *Turning Red* follows Mei (Rosalie Chiang) and her school friends on a quest to see the boyband 4*Town in concert. However, Mei has a secret of which she is ashamed: every time she gets overly excited, she turns into a giant red panda! The film's message, about puberty in teenagers, was beloved by audiences at home and adored by critics.

The three tracks Billie and
Finneas wrote exclusively
for the film were:

'Nobody Like U',

'1 True Love'
and
'U Know What's Up'.

The Sweet Smell of Success

Billie, in partnership with Parlux, broke into the affordable luxury fashion industry in 2021 with the release of her debut fragrance – **Eilish**. It is promoted on Billie's online store as a "scent for everyone", with aromas of vanilla, soft spices and cocoa. The perfume was such a success – with fans calling it the "ultimate Gen Z fragrance" – that Billie released two more.

Eilish 2 entrances with Italian bergamot, apple blossom and wild wet flowers, and is inspired by rain, trees and spices to evoke a mysterious and eerie feel.

Eilish 3 blends grapefruit, pink peppercorn and jasmine with a sexy heart notes of cedar, fir and saffron and base notes of amber and musk.

Time's Most Influential People in the World

The prestigious *Time* magazine included Billie as one of their most influential people in the world in 2021, an honour they award annually to creators and disrupters who make essential contributions to popular culture. Lil Nas X and Bad Bunny were the other notable musicians to also receive the same honour that year.

To give thanks to Billie and her incredible accomplishments – and still only 20 years old – Megan Thee Stallion, the Grammy-winning musical artist, wrote:

"Billie Eilish is a unique soul, with a voice, style and attitude all unapologetically her own. She is a rare spirit who speaks from her heart with no pretences."

No Time to Die

When Billie was just 18 years old, she was asked
by the James Bond producers to write and
perform a Bond theme for 2021's *No Time to Die*.
The previous youngest singer to record a Bond
theme was Sheena Easton, who was 22 years
old when she sang 'For Your Eyes Only' in 1981.

The song not only won Billie and Finneas their first Academy Award for Best Original Song in February 2022 – and made Billie the first person born in the 21st century to win an Academy Award – it was also the third Bond song in a row to win an Oscar following Adele's 'Skyfall' and Sam Smith's 'Writing on the Wall'.

Billie Eilish

B4 & After

The now-legendary belted-out note that Billie sings in the final verse of 'No Time to Die' (her Academy Award-winning James Bond theme) is a note that Billie had never delivered before in her music. It's a B4, FYI.

The note proved, if proof were necessary, that Billie could sing as big and as loud as any of her peers, such as Adele, Ariana Grande, Beyoncé, Dua Lipa or Selena Gomez. About the note, in December 2021, Billie told Chris Willman of *Variety*: "I had never done anything like that. It was really out of my comfort zone. I was worried that I wouldn't be able to do it, or that I wasn't good enough or people wouldn't like it. I didn't force it to be anything. It just became what it is."

Suffice to say audiences were hypnotized. As was James Bond himself, Daniel Craig, who described it as "fucking amazing". Billie responded by calling Daniel a "DILF"!

*

The Triple Crown

In March 2024, Billie and Finneas completed what is known as the Triple Crown – winning an Oscar, Grammy and Golden Globe – for the song 'What Was I Made For?' from the *Barbie* soundtrack. When the duo took the stage to be crowned for the final accolade at the Academy Awards on 10 March 2024, Eilish told the audience, "I had a nightmare about this last night," before taking a deep breath and bursting into laugher.

Billie then gave an impassioned speech with Finneas by her side:

"Thank you so much to the Academy. I just didn't think this would happen. I feel so incredibly lucky and honoured. Thank you to Greta Gerwig. I love you! Thank you for this. I'm so thankful for this song and for this movie, and the way that it made me feel. And this goes out to everyone who was affected by the movie and how incredible it is."

No. 1 Firsts
When her debut album came out in 2019, Billie was only 17 years old and she was the first artist born in the 2000s to have a No. 1 album (in 15 countries around the world including the US, UK, Australia and Canada) with *When We All Fall Asleep, Where Do We Go?*

Festival Firsts
She made history by being the youngest ever solo headlining act in the festival's history when she played Glastonbury's Pyramid Stage in 2022.

Grammy Firsts
She is the youngest artist in Grammy history to win all four general field categories: Record of the Year, Album of the Year, Song of the Year, as well as Best New Artist – all in the same year.

Streaming Firsts
A new-generation artist, she notched over 1 billion streams before even releasing her first album, allowing her to go from bedroom musician to global success.

"Words are more powerful than some noises. Noises won't last long. Lyrics are so important, and people don't realize that."

Billie, Parade.com, March 2023

Billie's Glastonbury Setlist
Somerset, UK, 24 June 2022

1. 'Bury A Friend'
2. 'I Didn't Change My Number'
3. 'NDA'
4. 'Therefore I Am'
5. 'My Strange Addiction'
6. 'idontwannabeyouanymore' / 'Lovely'
7. 'You Should See Me in a Crown'
8. 'Billie Bossa Nova'
9. 'Goldwing'
10. 'Oxytocin'
11. 'ilomilo'
12. 'Your Power'
13. 'Bellyache' / 'Ocean Eyes'
14. 'Getting Older'
15. 'Lost Cause'
16. 'When the Party's Over'
17. 'All the Good Girls Go to Hell'
18. 'Everything I Wanted'
19. 'Bad Guy'
20. 'Happier Than Ever'

Dreams & Nightmares

Billie's 2022 Glastonbury performance turned out to be one of the most important nights of her life. Not only did she become the youngest headline solo act in the festival's 50-year history, she also enticed more than 100,000 revellers to come see her 20-song set, one of the biggest attendances for the festival ever. She was 20.

Billie had performed before at Glastonbury, in 2019, and played to a 40,000-strong crowd. However, it wasn't until she headlined that she realized the magnitude of her popularity outside of the US.

What Billie Was Made For

Before Billie and Finneas wrote the haunting ballad 'What Was I Made For?', the duo genuinely believed that they had hit their critical and commercial peak and questioned whether they should continue writing songs. They had been struggling to write any good material for some time.

On a rainy January in 2023, on their first day back in the studio after they first saw *Barbie*, the pair were scratching their heads for song ideas. Then, Finneas suggested they try to write the *Barbie* assignment Greta Gerwig had given them. "I was like, 'What? You think after the day of garbage we've just made, we're going to make a perfect song for something that needs something really good?,'" Billie told a round table of peers for the *Hollywood Reporter*, in November 2023.

They did, and they wrote 'What Was I Made For?' in under 30 minutes, the quickest they have ever written a song! The song is now a modern classic.

"**My body is mine and yours is yours. Our own bodies are kind of the only real things which are truly ours.**"

Billie, interview with Jonathan Heaf
in *GQ*, 4 June 2020